God's World
Poetry for Teens

Sandy Bohon LMHC

Dedication

This book is dedicated to my two teenage grandchildren, Katie and Braden, and my preteen grandchild, Leland.

A Dream is Like a Star

A Dream is like a star
    That guides our thoughts at night,
They give our life much meaning
    Makes the future seem more bright.

But there can be a time
    That the star will burn away,
Our lives will seem pointless
    And dark will be our day.

To give our life new meaning
    The past behind is far,
We need to focus clearly
    Upon another star.

"Lift up your eyes and look to the heavens: who created all these? He who brings out the starry host one by one and calls forth each of them by name. Because of His great power and mighty strength, not one of them is missing."
(Isaiah 40:26)

Give Problems to God

Life is a maze of twists and turns
And things don't turn out right,
Through trying we seem helpless
In battles and dreams, we fight.

Something I wanted is gone
And another has taken its place,
Dreams and illusions, it sees
Like butterflies in meadows, we chase.

But in life, I finally learned
These problems to God I will give,
He'll see things will turn out right
And my life will be easy to live.

"Do not be anxious about anything, but in every situation, by prayer and petition, with thanksgiving, present your requests to God. And the peace of God, which transcends all understanding, will guard your hearts and minds in Christ Jesus." (Philippians 4:6,7)

Delusions

What could have been
Will never be
Open my eyes,
And help me see,
    Illusions -
    Delusions -
Are swirling around.

    My life is a haze,
    Like mice in a maze,
Deceptions abound -

Spiraling down
    Into the hole
I reached to God
    To save my soul.

"So do not fear for I am with you; do not be dismayed, for I am your God. I will strengthen you and help you; I will uphold you with My righteous right hand."
(Isaiah 41:10)

My Thoughts of you

I thought of you again tonight
While I was all alone,
The stars were twinkling in the sky
The moon so brightly shown.

And I called out to God above,
To hear my heartfelt plea,
To keep you safely in His care
And bring you back to me.

"May the Lord keep watch between you and me when
we are away from each other." (Genesis 31:49b)

God Made Me

The oceans, rivers, and lakes,
 The mountains and trees I see,
Were created by the hand of God
 Not by the will of me.

Birds flying high and lions roar,
 Wild horses on ranges run free,
Were created by the hand of God,
 Not by the will of me.

And before creation of the earth
 Christ in His foreknowledge could see,
That in a certain point in time
 He'd make a person as me.

"Remember the former things, those of long ago;
I am God, and there is no other; I am God, and
there is none like Me. I make known the end from
the beginning, from ancient times, what is still to
come, I say, 'My purpose will stand, and I will do
all that I please.'" (Isaiah 46:9,10)

My Dreams

As the leaf passes by in the streams
So my thoughts reflect on my dreams.
The reality of what will be,
Or the affect it has on me,
The blending of both it seems,
Allow me to continue my dreams.

"There is a time for everything, and a season
for every activity under the heavens; a time
to be born and a time to die, a time to plant
and a time to uproot... a time to weep and a
time to laugh, a time to mourn and a time to
dance." (Ecclesiastes 3:1,2,4)

Love is Like a Butterfly

Love is like a butterfly,
   Lighting here and there,
Very fickle in its flight
   With its love to share.

And like the butterfly,
   Lights many times a day,
In our lives, love touches us
   In many different ways.

So, do not be illusioned,
   Thinking love is what you're in,
'Cause tomorrow might bring another
   And your love will start again.

So, trust in God to help you see
   The one He has for you,
Where your souls can be one
   In a love that will be true.

"Trust in the Lord with all your heart and lean not on your own understanding; in all your ways submit to Him, and He will make your paths straight." (Proverbs 3:5,6)

Peace to All

I saw a duck swimming by
   The moon was just a sliver,
Birds were flying in the air
   As I sat beside the river.

The first star was shinning
   As darkness covered the air.
The glory of God was bringing
   Peace to all everywhere.

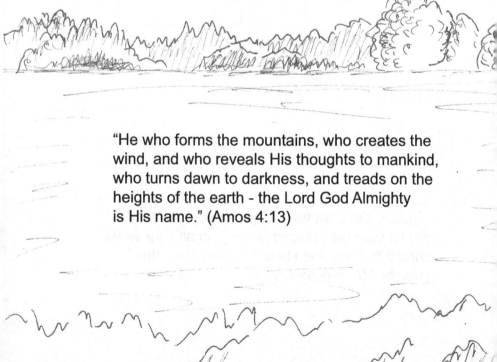

"He who forms the mountains, who creates the
wind, and who reveals His thoughts to mankind,
who turns dawn to darkness, and treads on the
heights of the earth - the Lord God Almighty
is His name." (Amos 4:13)

Floating Memories

A raindrop falls and disappears
And blends in with the pond,
Dreams are swirling in my mind,
Here and there and far beyond.

One day you're here, then you're gone,
All I have left are memories,
Of things we did, places seen
Softly floating in the breeze.

"The Lord is close to the brokenhearted
and saves those who are crushed in
spirit." (Psalm 34:18)

At Calvary

As leaves falling in the breeze
And softly hit the ground,
When my life on earth is over
My soul is heaven bound.

Not because I've been good,
But my life in Christ I place
Who died for me on Calvary,
And saved my by His grace.

"For it is by grace you have been saved, through faith - and this is not from yourselves, it is the gift of God - not by works, so that no one can boast." (Ephesians 2:8,9)

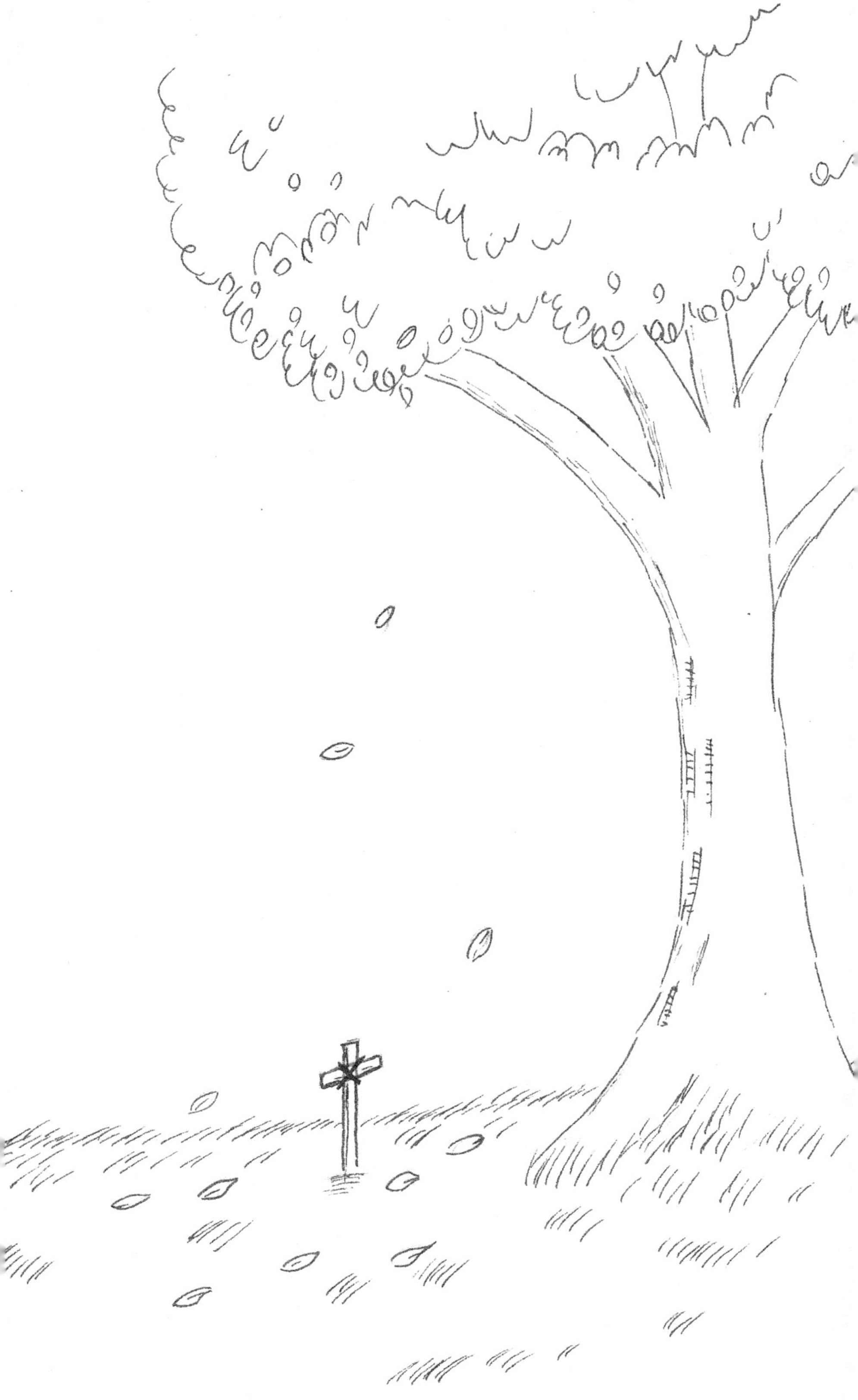

Burden of My Youth

God, I come in prayer tonight
　And open up my heart,
This heavy burden upon my soul
　Is tearing me apart.

When I was young, not long ago
　Warnings I did not heed,
In my folly, I went astray
　Upon pleasures, I did feed.

This but one mistake I made
　Was build upon the sand,
And like the cliffs by the sea
　It will always stand.

My life is still before me,
　Starting over cannot be done,
My prayer is not to erase the past
　Or from my life to run.

But like the ocean on the beach,
　Slowly washes the sand away,
Please fade this burden in my heart
　Until it's gone one day.

"For as high as the heavens are above the earth,
so great is His love for those who fear Him; as far
as the east is from the west, so far has He removed
our transgressions from us." (Psalm 103:11,12)

Whenever I'm not talking but I'm talking but not saying anything, it like goes through my head and I can hear it, but I didn't say anything.

Katie's Words

Talking in my head,
    The words swirling 'round,
Not touching the clouds
    Nor hitting the ground.

These words are mine
    Talking to me,
And when I speak to others,
    My words are set free.

God Loves me

I Love You

"May these words of my mouth and this
meditation of my heart, be pleasing in Your
sight, Lord, my Rock and my Redeemer."
(Psalm 19:14)

Tapping Rain

The rain is beating on my roof
    Drowning out the sound
Of a heart that has been broken
    Of a love that wasn't found.

All the miles between us
    And the time between each call
Hasn't decreased my feelings
    And to my knees I fall.

I pray to God to take away
    This never ending pain
So I can listen to the quiet,
    Of the tapping of the rain.

"The Lord is close to the brokenhearted and
saves those who are crushed in spirit."
(Psalm 34:18)

The Lord's Guiding

Lord, I know You love me
You take interest in my day,
And when I go adrift
You gently show me the way.

Of all life's little obstacles
And all my heart felt dreams,
You have always been right there
Walking beside me, it seems.

And looking into the future
I know You'll guide me along,
You'll surround me in Your love
And keep me where I belong.

"So that Christ may dwell in your hearts
through faith. And I pray that you, being
rooted and established in love, may have
power, together with all the Lord's holy
people, to grasp how wide and long and
high and deep is the love of Christ."
(Ephesians 3:17,18)

Drizzling Rain

Drizzle, drizzle goes the rain
As it hits my window pane.
Many thoughts are on my mind,
Some I should leave behind...
Many things I need to do,
Or maybe it's just a few.
But tomorrow is another day,
So, I think I'll sit and pray,
And I will dream and ponder,
Let my mind go 'round and yonder,
And enjoy the drizzling rain,
That softly hits my window pane.

"May these words of my mouth and this meditation of my heart be pleasing in Your sight, Lord, my Rock and my Redeemer." (Psalm 19:14)

Christ is the Only Way

Life on this earth is so short
And it is where we will decide
Where we spend eternity,
Will we in heaven abide?

Christ died on the cross for our sin
And He is the only way
That we can enter heaven
When we all die one day.

So, do not trust in yourselves
Or any good deed you may do
Nor any amount of money
Can ever help save you.

"For God so loved the world that He gave His one
and only Son, that whoever believes in Him shall
not perish but have eternal life." (John 3:16)

A Missionary

I am not rich by standards
In fact, I'm really quite poor,
My body grows weary from toiling
My feet from walking are sore.

Though it seems I have nothing,
My riches in heaven are placed,
Even if I had riches on earth
Only those in heaven would last.

"How, then, can they call on the one they have not believed in? And how can they believe in the one of whom they have not heard? And how can they hear without someone preaching to them? And how can anyone preach unless they are sent? As it is written, 'How beautiful are the feet of those who bring good news!'" (Romans 10:14,15)

Let My Light Shine

Lord give me the love to see
That we're all sinners saved by grace,
That someday in heaven we'll be
Where we'll see You face to face.

Lord give me the courage to tell
Others about how You died,
On the cross to save us from hell,
So in heaven, they can abide.

Lord give me the wisdom to live
A holy life for You each day,
So to others, I can give
A light to show them the way.

"Neither do people light a lamp and put it under
a bowl. Instead they put it on its stand, and it
gives light to everyone in the house. In the same
way, let your light shine before others, that they
may see your good deeds and glorify your
Father in heaven."(Matthew 5:15,16)

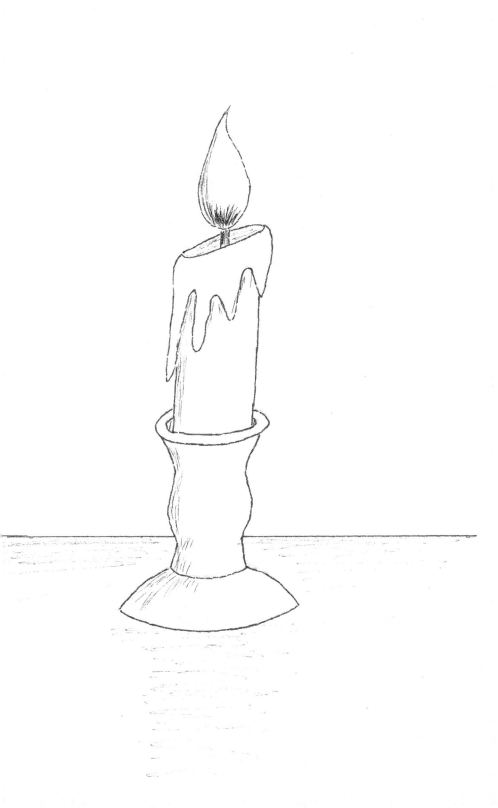

This Earthly Race

Lord, give me the faith to see
   And wisdom to understand,
That the future is to be lived
   As You have wisely planned.

Lord, give me the peace inside,
   That comes from trusting You,
Through You to live each day
   In everything I do.

Lord, help me keep my eyes above,
   My riches in heaven to place,
So that with joy I may run,
   This earthly human race.

"Brothers and sisters, I do not consider myself yet to have taken hold of it. But one thing I do: Forgetting what is behind and straining toward what is ahead, I press on toward the goal to win the prize for which God has called me heavenward in Christ Jesus." (Philppians 4:13,14)

Thoughts Before Marriage

So many people say they're in love,
    But all they do is fight,
Ups and downs, emotional rounds
    This can't be quite right.

Two people can say they're in love,
    And maybe they think they are,
Emotional trips and games they play,
    Their love lacks much by far.

True love is when someone puts,
    The other first in their life,
True love is a bond of peace
    Wherein there is no strife.

So, if you think you're in love,
    And your life's turned inside out,
Reconsider the mess you're in
    And start looking 'round about.

For there is someone out there,
    Who'll love you with all their heart,
They'll be kind and treat you well,
    Find them and never part.

"For this reason a man will leave his father and mother and be united to his wife, and the two will become one flesh." (Ephesians 5:31)

Feeling Sad

I woke up today feeling sad
   And I didn't know why,
My heart was so heavy,
   My life passing me by.

I get into these moods
   Feeling sad, anxiety,
Of regrets from the past,
   Or what the future will bring.

Then I thought of Jesus
   And all He's done for me,
He tells us to be content
   And live worry free.

If we are praising Jesus
   Filling our heart with song,
There's no room for sadness,
   Praising Him all day long.

"Rejoice in the Lord always, I will say it again: Rejoice!" (Philippians 4:4)

"Give thanks in all circumstances; for this is God's will for you in Christ Jesus." (1 Thessalonians 5:18)

Lazarus and the Rich Man

I am just Lazarus
For food, I have to beg,
I've only got one coat
And sores upon my leg.

I see the rich man
Pass me by each day,
When I ask for alms
He turns and walks away.

And when I had died
In the grave, I was laid,
The rich man also died
Respects to him were paid.

But now I'm in Paradise
No longer am I poor,
For I had believed in Christ
When He knocked upon my door.

"Jesus answered, 'I am the way and the truth and the life. No one comes to the Father except through me.'" (John 14:6)

My Redeemer

My Redeemer came to earth,
    To shed His blood for me,
Though I'm the one who sinned
    On the cross, He died for me.

And Satan could not stop,
    No matter how he tried,
Christ hung upon that cross
    For me that day, He died.

If I lose my life on earth
    My treasures in heaven I place,
My life will not be in vain
    When I see him face to face.

"Do not store up for yourselves treasures
on earth, where moths and vermin destroy,
and where thieves break in and steal. But
store up for yourselves treasures in heaven,
where moths and vermin do not destroy,
and where thieves do not break in and steal.
For where your treasure is, there your heart
will be also." (Matthew 6:19-21)

Burden for the Lost

Lord help me to have
A burden for the lost,
That I will win souls
No matter the cost.

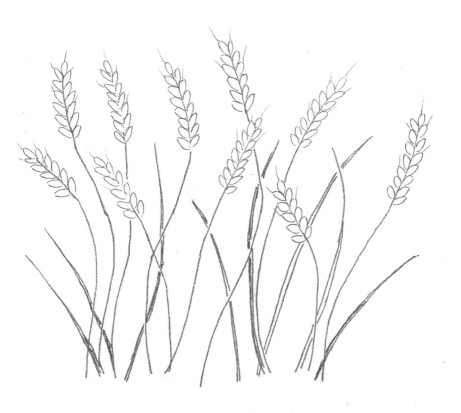

"Don't you have a saying, 'It's still four months
until harvest'? I tell you, open your eyes and
look at the fields! They are ripe for harvest."
(John 4:35)

Mirror Mirror

Mirror mirror on the wall
Who's the fairest of them all?
   Let me see
   It said to me.
I see mountains and rivers grand,
I see people all over the land.
   People tall
   Others small.
Why do you ask me to compare,
You with others everywhere?
   God made you
   And others too.
So be content with who you are,
Put Jesus first and you'll go far.

"For you created my inmost being; You knit me together in my mother's womb. I praise You because I am fearfully and wonderfully made; Your works are wonderful, I know that full well." (Psalm 139:13,14)

Joint Heirs with Christ

Though I am but flesh and blood
My life a passing flower,
In eternal time this life is brief
Like a summer shower.

And though I was but nothing
Upon Christ's payment, I did believe,
Now I've become joint heirs with Christ
Eternal life in heaven to receive.

"The Spirit Himself testifies with our spirit
that we are God's children. Now if we are
children, then we are heirs - heirs of God
and co-heirs with Christ, if indeed we share
in His sufferings in order that we may also
share in His glory." (Romans 8:16,17)

New Day

As the mist rises in the morning
And the sun brings in a new day,
Fill me Lord with Your blessing,
Keep me in Your will, I pray.

"Do not conform to the pattern of this world, but be
transformed by the renewing of your mind. Then
you will be able to test and approve what God's
will is - His good, pleasing and perfect will."
(Romans 12:2)

Cast Your Burdens Upon God

Many times problems arise,
   And I come to a fork in the road,
My body grows, oh so weary,
   Carrying my heavy load.

And it seems that just this once
   I'll stumble and fall to the side,
As the road grows oh so narrow,
   That once was big and wide.

But at the fork, I hear a voice
   From God away up high,
Cast all your burdens upon Me
   And I will help you by.

And then I think of all the troubles,
   That God has helped me through,
He is willing to guide us along
   If only we'll ask Him to.

"Come to Me, all you who are weary and burdened, and I will give you rest. Take My yoke upon you and learn from Me, for I am gentle and humble in heart, and you will find rest for your souls. For My yoke is easy and my burden is light." (Matthew 11:28-30)

Why

Why was I born on this earth
What purpose is there for me,
I feel my wheels keep spinning
Like waves on an endless sea.

Even though I'm a Christian
I feel life's passing me by,
And so, I will turn to God
And silently ask Him why.

I know He has the answer,
Reading God's Word, I did find,
'Trust in me, and you will know
One day on the other side.'

"And we know that in all things God works
for the good of those who love Him, who
have been called according to His purpose."
(Romans 8:28)

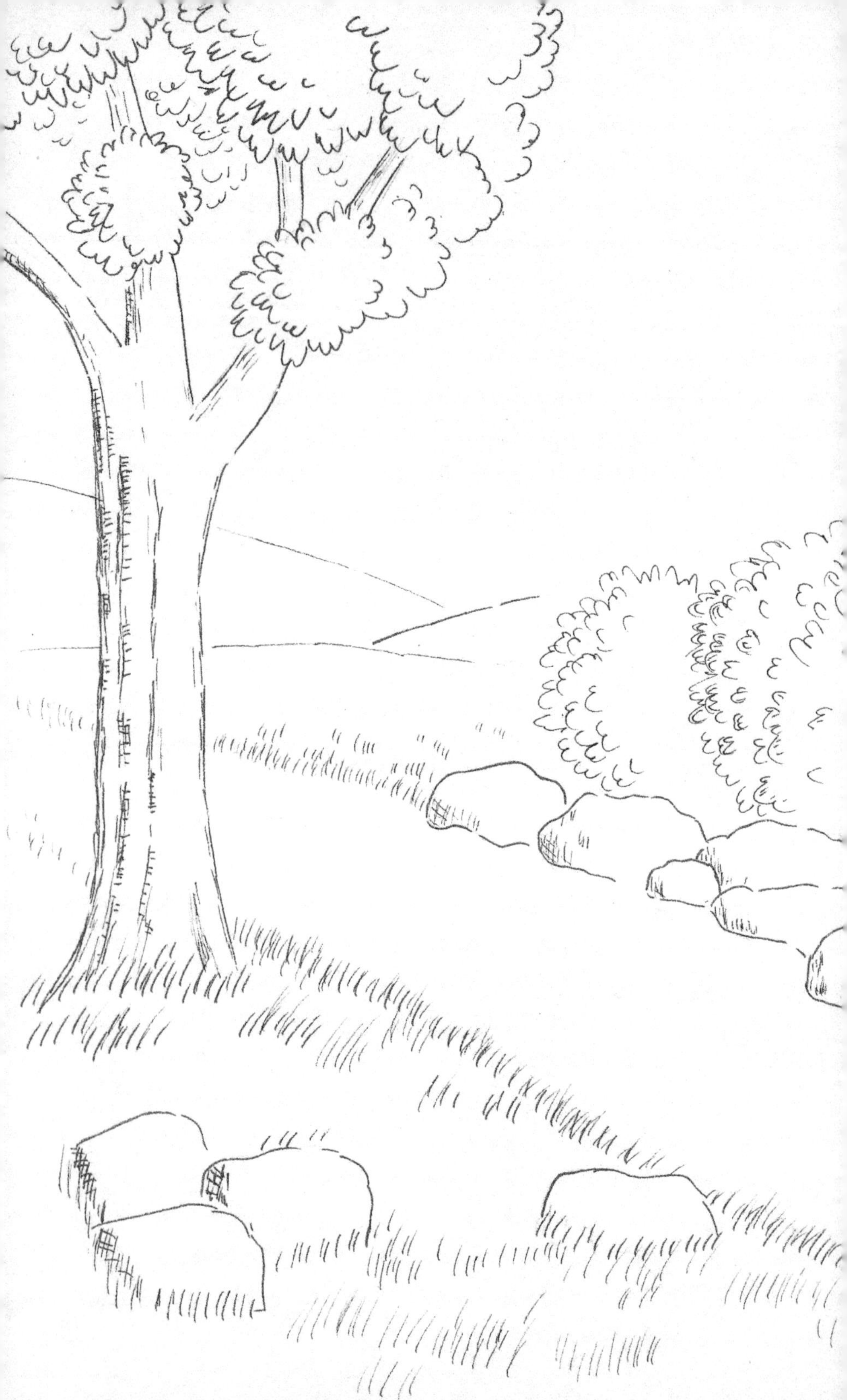

Choose Your Friends

A friend is like a path
They can lead you right or wrong,
They can tear your values down,
Or help you be more strong.

A friend's words throw weight
Upon what you think or do,
So when you pick your friends
Think of their effect on you.

Will your friend help you grow
In morals and in the Lord,
For if they bring you down
Their friendship you can't afford.

So pray to God to send you
Good friends to walk beside,
And give you the courage
To cast others on the side.

"Blessed is the one who does not walk in
step with the wicked or stand in the way
that sinners take or sit in the company of
mockers, but whose delight is in the law
of the Lord, and who meditates on His law
day and night." (Psalm 1:1,2)

Christmas Time

I love Christmas time of the year,
    When the lights are out at night,
It reminds me of Jesus' birth
    When the star was shining bright.

The angels sang up in the sky
    While the shepherds were in the field.
The shepherds went to see Jesus,
    And they praised God as they kneeled.

The Maji saw the star up high,
    Which they followed to Bethlehem.
There they gave gifts to Jesus,
    And bowed to worship Him.

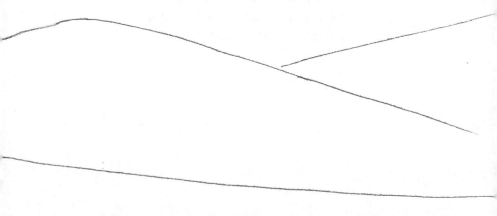

"But the angel said to them, 'Do not be afraid, I bring you good news that will cause great joy for all the people. Today in the town of David a Savior has been born to you; He is the messiah, the Lord.'"
(Luke 2:10,11)

Open Doors

Life is a maze of unopened doors
That we pass through one by one,
Through some, we stop and ponder
Through others, we want to run.

Each door slowly opens to us
And we quickly chance inside,
Will we enjoy this season?
Or do we want to hide?

No matter what each door brings
It will soon be left behind,
We pray that God will bless us
And sweet memories we will find.

"Praise be to the God and Father of our
Lord Jesus Christ, who has blessed us in
the heavenly realms with every spiritual
blessing in Christ. For He chose us in Him
before the creation of the world to be holy
and blameless in His sight."
(Ephesians 1:3,4)

Negative People

Many people are negative
Their thoughts are dark and gloom,
There is no joy in their life
Like dead bodies in a tomb.

They spread their negative thoughts
On all that they're around,
Like poison in a serpent
Their evil does abound.

But they'll have a day of judgment,
And Karma can be cruel.
So don't be a negative person
And live by the golden rule.

"So in everything, do to others what you would
have them do to you." (Matthew 7:12a)

Children of Light

There is a gulf between darkness and light,
Between Satan and following the Lord,
There is a ship that sets out to sea,
That all Christians should be aboard.

The earth left behind is the darkness,
The ship out to sea is the light,
The earth is the world and its pleasures,
Where Satan, his demons do fight.

We shouldn't live our lives in the world,
For in Christ we are children of light,
By leaving the world in darkness behind,
We live in the ship of God's might.

"For you were once darkness, but now you are
in the Lord. Live as children of light (for the fruit
of the light consists in all goodness, righteousness
and truth) and find out what pleases the Lord."
(Ephesians 5:8-10)

Daily Read God's Word

Too busy in my life I was
To read God's Word every day,
My many friends and commitments
Took me from the Lord to stray.

And when I got in trouble
Not a way out could I see,
Then I turned to God for help
And, by His grace, He helped me.

For through the Bible we learn
True life and how to live,
And if we follow carefully
Blessings to us, God will give.

"Your word is a lamp for my feet, a light
on my path." (Psalm 119:105)

Your Will Lord

All blessing that
　　You give,
Within my soul
　　To live.

Your will Lord,
　　I seek,
Within my heart
　　To keep.

Love You've shown
　　My way,
Keeps me through
　　Each day.

Your will Lord
　　Not mine,
Is etched across
　　The time.

"You alone are the Lord. You made the heavens, even the
highest heavens, and all their starry host, the earth and
all that is on it, the seas and all that is in them. You give
life to everything, and the multitudes of heaven worship
You." (Nehemiah 9:6)

God speaks to us through His Bible and through nature. Being out in nature is awesome and relaxing. The Bible speaks about how God created the heavens and earth, and He created them for us to enjoy.

God gave us the Bible so that we can learn about Him and His will for our lives. It also speaks about how we are all sinners, and from the creation of the world, God prepared a way to restore fellowship that was broken from Adam and Eve's sin.

Jesus came to earth to die on the cross for our sins in our place. Salvation is trusting in the payment that Christ made on the cross in our place. When you trust Jesus as your Savior, as a free gift, you can spend eternity with Him.

"I write these things to you who believe in the name of the Son of God so that you may know that you have eternal life."
(1John 5:13 NIV)

About the Author

Sandy Bohon is a Licensed Mental Health Counselor practicing in central Florida. She received her Bachelor's degree from Florida Bible College and a Master of Counseling degree from Liberty University. In her spare time, Sandy enjoys spending time with her family, going to the beach and gardening.

Other books by Sandy Bohon available on Amazon:

- ~ Joy in Overcoming Depression Through God's Word
- ~ JOY in Knowing Jesus Through God's Word
- ~ Poetry and Devotions for the Soul
- ~ Poetry and Devotions for the Soul for Youth
- ~ God's World Nature Poems
- ~ God's World Family Poems and Prayers

For more information please contact me:
    sandybohonlmhc@gmail.com
And join my mailing list at
    www.sandybohonlmhc.com

If you enjoyed this book please leave a a review on Amazon. Thanks!

Made in the USA
Monee, IL
01 February 2025

11413546R00039